Reach for the Son

A Collection of Devotions & Prayers

Kristen West

Author photos by Hannah Taylor.

Cover photo © 2025 by Kristen West. All rights reserved.

Copyright © 2025 by Kristen West. All rights reserved.

Published by The Spotted Feather, an imprint of Colorful Crow Publishing.

(PB) ISBN: 978-1-964271-24-8

(eBook) ISBN: 978-1-964271-25-5

To Rosemund Gleason and Marjorie Hendra—

Who first taught me the value of words and the power behind them. I smile knowing you are now in the arms of Jesus, where the reaching you began on this earth has been made complete in His presence.

Introduction

I used to think I could do life alone, needing no one and foolishly thinking I was self-sufficient.

Truth be told, those days left me feeling more empty, isolated, and unseen than my pride would care to admit.

I'm grateful for my Savior's patience.

Over the years, it has become abundantly apparent how very much I need community.

We all do. God made us that way.

And God has used a multitude of people over the course of my life to encourage, inspire, and challenge me as I walk out my faith journey.

These precious individuals have taken time to share Scriptures with me, texted me out-of-the-blue to say God brought me to their minds and they're praying for me, or sat with me in some hard seasons and deep valleys to simply remind me that I'm not alone and that God cares.

I am forever grateful for the mark each one of them has made on my life.

It is my prayer that this book would intersect your life in that kind of meaningful way. I don't believe it's an accident that you're reading it.

I pray that its contents would help you see Jesus more clearly – no matter what season of life you're going through – and that you would remember He sees you; He loves you; and He cares for you.

Sometimes we just need another voice in our life to point us to Him.

A voice that reminds us, once again, of our purpose ...

We were created to be dependent on Jesus. We were made to consistently reach for the Son!

Reaching with you!

Contents

A Life Lesson from My Honeymoon

You do not have because you do not ask.
James 4:2 (NIV)

My husband and I view vacations a little differently. Quiet retreats, historical museums, and plenty of time away from anything else that breathes is his idea of a great getaway. Mine? The more rollercoasters, entertainment, and people you can pack into it, the better!

Needless to say, our honeymoon was a devastating disappointment. Not because Anthony didn't try to make it wonderful, romantic, and completely memorable, but because he couldn't read my mind and I didn't bother to let him know what I preferred.

He even asked in advance, "Where would you enjoy going on our honeymoon?" My rose-colored-glasses, dreamy-eyed response was, "Ohhh, you choose."

(*Didn't he just **know** I would want to go on a Caribbean cruise!?*)

Our honeymoon was not spent cruising, though. Instead we spent the first nine days of wedded bliss on an exhausting, non-stop road trip that took us from the mountains of Northern Georgia to some of New England's best historical hotspots (think Paul Revere, the Revolutionary War, and the Boston Tea Party).

Yawn

(Don't get me wrong, I appreciate history – just not on my honeymoon.)

I was crushed.

My poor husband was confused and heartbroken. From his standpoint, he had put together the crème de la crème of trips and couldn't understand why his new wife wasn't as overjoyed as he was.

We laugh about it now, but it was a lesson that served to be foundational moving forward – in our marriage and spiritually.

I didn't receive the honeymoon I longed for because I didn't ask. Plain and simple.

My husband would have done everything in his power to provide me with a honeymoon trip that made me happy, but I prevented it by keeping my mouth shut and not specifically asking for what I really wanted.

How often do we do that with God?

How many times do we want or need something yet neglect to pray about it and just hope God will make it turn out the way we want?

Matthew 7:7 makes it clear, *"Ask, and it will be given to you ... "*

He longs to be in relationship with us and part of any good relationship is communication.

He waits patiently to hear what's on our minds, troubling our hearts, or vexing our souls. And all the while, He invites us to speak up and share our requests with Him.

Let's talk to Him ...

Father, teach me to bring everything to you. The wants and the needs. The big and the small. Help me to see how much you enjoy our conversations and are always ready to talk. Thank you for always listening and hearing my heart. Amen.

Can't Seem to Catch a Break

Do not worry about tomorrow; for tomorrow will worry
about itself. Each day has enough trouble of its own.
Matthew 6:34 (AMP)

Have you ever asked yourself the question: *"What else could possibly go wrong?"*

Anthony and I had one of those weeks where all we could do was look at each other, laugh, and ask that very question.

A pipe under our bathroom sink had burst; our refrigerator was leaking on the kitchen floor; and the A/C in one of our vehicles went on the fritz.

On top of that, we were trying to reconcile a fraudulent charge we discovered on one of our credit cards; chase a few contractors for some home repair quotes; and help some dear friends who were navigating a very challenging season of life.

Calgon, take me away!

There was a time when, as a young Christ-follower, I believed that my new life with Jesus would somehow shield me from the day-to-day problems and frustrations of this world.

My thought was: new life in Jesus = joy and happiness for the rest of my life.

It may sound silly, but I've found that this mentality can be a common misunderstanding among many Christ-followers.

Why else would we be tempted to lose our peace and joy when temporary troubles arise?

Why else would we be so quick to question God's love for us when we encounter daily problems in life?

But, the truth will set us free.

And the truth is that *"no more grief, crying, or pain"* is a promise for heaven, not earth (Revelation 21:4 CSB).

In John 16, Jesus told His disciples plainly, *"Here on earth you will have many trials and sorrows. But take heart, because I have overcome the world."* (vs. 33 NLT)

Life is filled to the brim with disappointments, setbacks, and general maintenance issues. It is essential for us to remember these truths from Scripture so that we don't lose hope, become discouraged, weary, or frustrated in our faith.

We are not promised deliverance from problems this side of eternity. What we are promised, however, is that Jesus Himself will walk with us through every single one.

"The Lord Himself goes before you and will be with you; He will never leave you nor forsake you. Do not be afraid; do not be discouraged." (Deuteronomy 31:8 NIV)

Every problem today is an opportunity to reach for Jesus. Ask Him for help; lean on Him for guidance, clarity, and provision.

Don't worry, He's got you. Everything will be okay.

Jesus, this life can be so hard. You see the pain I'm feeling even now; the trials that I'm facing today; and the troubles that seem to be endless. Please give me grace to move forward with you as I believe your word and trust that you are always faithful. You will guide me through these challenging seasons every step of the way. Amen.

Dealing with Mental Clutter

... taking every thought captive to obey Christ.
2 Corinthians 10:5 (HCSB)

We all do it, don't we?

In the hustle and bustle of our day-to-day activities, we throw things in closets or drawers, pile stuff on counter spaces, or toss things into random nooks and crannies thinking, *I'll get to that soon.*

Days turn into months. Months grow into years. Suddenly, we realize these catch-all spaces need attention, cleaning, and some organizational TLC.

Not too long ago, I found myself embarking on a few organizational projects including cleaning out some closets and sifting through filing cabinets jam-packed with outdated and unnecessary papers.

While my paper shredder was on the verge of work overload and heat exhaustion, I wondered how many times my mind (and consequently, my heart) have looked like my neglected home office files and crowded closets?

It can be so easy to walk through our day flinging our thoughts into a mental corner.

As a result, our minds begin to pile up with unchecked burdens, worries, and baggage that threaten to overwhelm us simply because we didn't put them in the proper place to begin with.

Before too long, we realize we feel fearful, worried, empty, dry, exhausted, lonely (the list goes on and on) and we wonder what happened.

Romans 12:2 gives us clear direction when dealing with mental clutter.

"And do not be conformed to this world [any longer with its superficial values and customs], but be transformed and progressively changed [as you mature spiritually] by the renewing of your mind ... "(AMP)

Having our minds *"transformed and progressively changed"* is an ongoing, daily, organizational mental discipline.

Permitting wrong thinking, lies, or ideas contrary to the Bible to clutter up space in our heads is detrimental to our well-being and adversely impacts our walk with Jesus and our ability to love our neighbor as well.

It takes just a moment to march that dirty sock over to the hamper and throw it in – but, it does take effort and intentionality.

How much easier is it on laundry day, though, to have everything in the hamper ready to go rather than franticly canvasing the house playing hide-and-seek with dirty clothes?

The same is true with our thoughts. Examine them as they come in and take them captive. Hold them up to the Word of God to see if they need to be filed or trashed.

The more we do this, the more clutter-free our mind (and, ultimately, our heart) will be enabling us to think more clearly and love more deeply!

Jesus, examining my thoughts can feel so hard to do sometimes! Please help me learn how to process the things going through my mind and teach me to separate what's true from what's not. Teach me to line my thoughts up with your word. As I do, I thank you for guarding my heart and mind with your peace that passes all understanding. Amen.

Does Your Life Feel Like It's Falling Apart?

For what is seen is temporary, but what is unseen is eternal. 2 Corinthians 4:18 (HCSB)

The Big Island of Hawaii is home to a phenomenal tree called the 'ohi'a lehua.

This tree flourishes in an environment that looks extraterrestrial. Hardened black lava from former Kilauea eruptions cover the landscape. The surface of the land looks as barren, harsh, and uninviting as can be.

It's in these conditions that the ʻohiʻa lehua tree exists.

This tree grows where no other tree does because it has learned to close its pores to the toxic gases that are expelled during a volcanic eruption. The dangerous gases spewed during Kilauea's flare-ups don't phase the ʻohiʻa lehua because it just holds its breath.

Where other trees are destroyed by this climate of opposition, the ʻohiʻa lehua thrives.

2 Corinthians offers us a glimpse into Paul's life – who, like the ʻohiʻa lehua, was no stranger to resistance.

As he walked out the Gospel-centered life God had called him to and actively demonstrated Christ's love wherever he went, Paul wasn't always received with open arms (or hearts).

He and his team of disciple-makers were *"... afflicted in every way but not crushed; ... perplexed but not in despair; ... struck down but not destroyed."* (Chapter 4:8 – 9 CSB)

Doesn't exactly sound like the kind of life folks would jump in line to sign up for, right?

But Paul understood what God is working to teach all of us who follow Him – opposition is a catalyst for growth.

"... we're not giving up ... even though on the outside it often looks like things are falling apart on us, on the inside, where God is making new life, not a day goes by without His unfolding grace." (vs. 16 MSG)

Does your life feel like it's falling apart?

Anything from relationship fails to flat tires; unexpected illnesses to job uncertainties can serve to drive us into the arms of King Jesus and help make us more like Him, if we let it.

The question is, are we?

Like the 'ohi'a lehua, are we willing to let the opposition in our lives serve as opportunities for growth? Are we willing to allow it to shape us to look more like Jesus?

If so, we have a promise for such difficult seasons (and an incredible hope).

"For our momentary light affliction is producing for us an absolutely incomparable eternal weight of glory." (vs. 17 CSB)

Jesus, you see the difficulties I'm facing today. Thank you for helping me to remember that they are temporary. They will end. Please use this season to help me look more like you. Help me to flourish in the face of opposition and thrive like the 'ohi'a lehua tree as I put my trust in you. Amen.

Having Trouble Hearing God?

Yet [Jesus] often withdrew to deserted places and prayed.
Luke 5:16 (HCSB)

I couldn't hear a word he was saying.

My husband was an entire room away and trying to talk to me as I was getting ready for bed. At the moment, all I could hear was the whir of the electric tooth brush in my mouth, the water draining in the sink, and the television chatter in the background.

I spit the toothpaste out, slid the toothbrush back on its charger, and yelled, *"Just a second. I can't hear you!"*

After drying my hands, I walked over to where he was so I could understand what he was trying to tell me.

The solution to my hearing problem in this situation was obvious. I had to remove the noise; get closer to the source; and listen.

Yet, somehow it hasn't always felt that obvious whenever I'm wondering why I'm not hearing from God.

Maybe you can relate?

James 4:8 says, *"Draw near to God, and He will draw near to you."* (HCSB)

The typical busyness of our days doesn't offer much in the way of quiet. We tend to fill every waking moment from sun-up to sun-down with activities, appointments, and plans.

God's not interested in competing with all of that for our attention.

It's our choice to position ourselves so that we can hear Him.

Unless we're purposeful to take time and draw near to God, the world's cacophony of loud noises and numerous demands will always drown out His quiet, still voice.

Jesus wasn't immune to it, either.

He made a practice of slipping away from the hullabaloo of life to be alone with God (Mark 1:35; Luke 6:12; Matthew 14:13).

Jesus understood that in order to hear His Father's voice clearly, He had to draw near, eliminate the external noise, and listen.

A truth so simple we see it in action in our everyday lives with our spouses, our kids, and our friends.

How much more should we apply it to our Heavenly Father who has the words of life for our daily needs?

Father, help me slow down to draw near to You today. Let the world be silenced so I can begin to hear more clearly what You're whispering to me. Amen.

May my prayer be set before You like incense …

Psalm 141:2 (HCSB)

Today, Lord Jesus …
I choose to serve You and lay down my life.
I love You and worship You with every breath that is in me.
Help me remember that You are good –
all the time; in every circumstance.
When I don't know where to turn or what to do, I choose You.
You are God; I am not.

Today, Lord Jesus …
I give you my heart, my life, my family, and my deepest longings.
You know me better than I know myself.
You see my worries, fears, failures, and pride.
Forgive me for all the times I've clung to my sin instead of to You.
I surrender everything to You.

Today, Lord Jesus …
Let my life positively impact those I meet.
Let them glimpse eternity in me.
Let my words, my actions, my silence, and my tone all point to Jesus.
The Hope of the world.
The Source of abundant life.

Today, Lord Jesus …
I lay down my prejudices and my biases.
I release the notion that things have to go my way.
I don't have Your perfect vantage point.
I am ignorant of how Your divine wisdom is beautifully at work.
I defer to Your omniscience.

Today, Lord Jesus …
Take my brokenness and redeem it.
Use it in a way that brings You glory.
Help me see those who feel unseen and invisible.
Let me be a conduit of love.
Let me be a vessel of Your truth and grace.

Today, Lord Jesus …
My life is a prayer.
I pour it out.
A living sacrifice.
Let it be acceptable to You.
Amen.

Help for a Reckless Mouth

The one who guards his mouth and tongue keeps himself out of trouble. Proverbs 21:23 (CSV)

Working in HR, I see the enormous impact of people's words, including my own. Our words can skew a narrative; affirm someone's confidence; or infuse personal emotions into situations that complicate the actual matter at hand.

Our words have the power to bring clarity or cause a lot of trouble.

Learning how to guard what comes out of our mouth is probably one of the biggest challenges we have as human beings.

God knew this would be a problem for us and, in His wisdom, provides truth so that we can learn how to control our reckless-prone mouths.

"The more you talk, the more likely you are to sin. If you are wise, you will keep quiet." (Proverbs 10:19 GNT)

"The mind of the righteous person thinks before answering ... " (Proverbs 15:28 CSV)

These verses are so clear and simple, aren't they? Yet, we read them and might think, *"Easier said than done!"*

But like many other things, the discipline of learning to control our mouths takes time. It's not something that will happen overnight.

Our willingness to be obedient, however, is.

If we recognize we have a runaway mouth problem, are we willing to admit it? If so, are we willing to surrender it and submit ourselves to God and His Word to become more mature, kind, and gracious in how we use our words?

That, my friends, is the key.

Our mouth is the conduit for what is already in our hearts.

"The mouth speaks what the heart is full of." (Matthew 12:34 NIV)

Surrendering our mouths ultimately begins with surrendering our hearts.

Doing this invites God into our lives to do His life-changing, grace-filling, reckless-mouth saving work that only He can do.

And then, He promises to help us learn how to speak and use our words in a life-giving way.

"... Who placed a mouth on humans? ... I will help you speak and I will teach you what to say." (Exodus 4:11 & 12 CSV)

Jesus, help me guard my mouth as I learn to be slow to speak and quick to hear. Teach me to use my words to build up and not tear down, to bring life and encouragement to others. May the words that come out of my mouth be a blessing to you always as well as the those around me. Amen.

When it Feels like Life is Going Backwards

God works so that people will be in awe of Him.
Ecclesiastes 3:14 (CSB)

Have you ever felt like you're going backwards in life? Try as you may to move forward, it just seems like progress is unattainable and the only direction destined for you is reverse?

I cannot tell you how many times I've felt that way!

One of my more obvious examples comes from early on in my marriage. Anthony and I headed to the altar wholeheartedly ready to merge our lives into a blissful union but the first several years of wedded life had us wondering when the "worse" part of "for better or worse" was going to end.

We spent years at each other's throats before we sincerely began to understand just how lovingly God was working.

Ecclesiastes 3 says, *"There is an occasion for everything, and a time for every activity under heaven ... "*

"... a time to plant and a time to uproot ... a time to tear down and a time to build ... " (vs. 1-3 CSB)

As newlyweds, Anthony and I assumed there would be hurdles to overcome, but we never imagined we'd have things that needed to be uprooted or torn down. Ideologies, bad theologies, and a few other personal-ologies needed to be unpacked, processed, and thrown out.

Much of who we were, as people, needed to be unlearned.

It felt like we were going backwards! I lost count of the times where I truly thought the rest of our lives were going to be spent slogging through hopeless days fraught with tension and endless nights filled with tears.

We slowly began to realize that in order for God to build the healthy, strong, and unified foundation in our marriage that He wanted for us, it was necessary to deal with the toxic, bad, and unhealthy things that we'd brought with us into our union.

Interestingly enough, I've seen this principle in many other areas of my life – work, raising children, navigating friendships.

It's the times when I feel like I'm going backwards the most that God is actively at work uprooting and tearing down bad thinking, sin habits, and selfish tendencies in me.

He's quietly but patiently working to craft my heart to look like His and fashion and build my character to be more like Jesus.

And, ultimately, He gets all the glory! I don't. He does the incredible, life-changing work! I don't.

And, He intentionally works so that we will be in awe of Him because no one else can do what He does!

Jesus, help me to see you at work in my life today – moving me forward even if it looks to the contrary. I surrender my unbelief to you and ask that you would open my eyes and help me see the marvelous things you are already doing on my behalf. Amen.

Is there Purpose in Pain?

I am the vine; you are the branches. John 15:5 (NIV)

Why do bad things happen to good people?

Honestly, there's not one simple answer to that question – the question is complex and so is the answer.

I Corinthians 13:12 reminds us that while we're in these mortal bodies, *"we see things imperfectly"* – not clearly.

It's as though we're squinting in a fog.

Compounding that is the fact that we live in a broken world where sin and evil still exist.

That said, this side of Heaven, we will never have *all* the answers to many of our hard questions; however, as Christ-followers we have complete assurance that our Father does.

And that He loves us.

And cares for us.

However, John 15: 1 – 2 offers us *an* answer to that challenging question.

"I am the true vine, and my Father is the gardener ... He prunes every branch that produces fruit so that it will produce more fruit." (CSB)

Here, Jesus referred to God as the gardener, Himself as the vine, and those of us who follow Him as branches.

A skilled gardener understands that pruning is necessary for the health of the plant. However, if we interviewed the plant, I'm not so sure it would agree.

Pruning involves cutting away.

I imagine the plant would therefore see this process as a painful one and chalk it up as a bad thing.

It may even question the motive of the gardener and wonder how he might bring himself to be so cruel.

The plant might think things like:

I thought the gardener loved me?

If the gardener cared for me, why would he permit this pain in my life?

Can I even trust the gardener?

Yet, all the while, the gardener knows that pruning is necessary for the prosperity of the plant.

In order for the plant to thrive and be healthy, dead vines need to be cut back, diseased limbs need to be removed, and excess foliage cut off.

The gardener prunes the plant because he wants it to flourish.

He prunes the plant because he cherishes and cares for it.

He prunes the plant so that it will grow and be healthier than ever before.

There's purpose in the pruning.

My friend, today if you find yourself wrestling with why "bad things" may be happening to you, I pray that you will remember the kind and loving gardener.

The "bad things" in our lives ultimately have purpose – even when we don't see clearly or understand why in the moment.

Lord Jesus, I acknowledge that I don't see things as clearly as you do. I trust you with my life and thank you for your faithful pruning that, ultimately, is making way in me for fresh growth and ever-increasing fruitfulness. Amen.

Reaching for the Son

Let your light so shine before men, that they may see your good works, and glorify your Father which is in heaven. Matthew 5:16 (KJV)

I was taking a leisurely walk through the woods and came upon a large patch of bright, yellow wildflowers.

The sun was getting high in the sky and, being the photo-obsessed person that I am, I couldn't help but stop to capture a few artistic images of the beautiful scene.

As I kneeled and crouched here and there to get the perfect pictures, I noticed something unique about the flowers – they all seemed to be reaching for the sunshine.

Their stems were stretched in unison towards the light; their faces almost smiling as they basked in the rays of the sun's brilliance.

Their carefree example spoke to my heart and reminded me again of my one true calling in this life – I was created to reach for the Son.

A truth so simple yet so overlooked sometimes when it comes to daily victory in my faith walk.

No matter the worry, care, or frustration, my primary responsibility is (and always will be) to look to Jesus.

Because it's there, soaking in His presence, that I find peace.

It's there, gazing on His glory, that I find strength.

And it's there, basking in His warmth and light, that I am changed more into His likeness.

Psalm 34:5 says it this way, *"Those who look to Him are radiant ... "* (HCSB)

To be radiant is to shine brightly or to send out light. And, isn't that God's purpose for us as His image-bearers?

As much as we may try, we will never be radiant or shine brightly through human determination, gritting of our teeth, or any amount of willpower.

It simply requires sitting in the glorious presence of the Son – faces tilted upwards; our whole being reaching for Heaven.

Like the beautiful flowers in the field.

As Walt Whitman once said, *"Keep your face always toward the sunshine – and shadows will fall behind you."*

Father, I take a moment right now to gaze on the Son. Your Son, Jesus. The One whose glory and honor I live for today. Let my face be radiant as I consider all that He's done for me and may my heart truly reflect His brilliance today as I let my light shine for you. Amen.

The Remedy for Spiritual Amnesia

... the Spirit of truth ... will guide you into all the truth.
John 16:13 (CSB)

Reminders.

We have them set on our phones, in our cars, and on our computers these days, don't we?

A brilliant addition to our electronics, reminders are a great way to help ensure we are giving attention to those things we don't want to forget.

But what about spiritual reminders? Those things that can't be set on a device or using an app.

In John 14, Jesus is having a conversation with His disciples. He is aware that His time on earth is coming to a close and is spending the last little bit of it encouraging these 12 men.

His conversation includes important bullet points, promises, and prayers.

Then, in verse 26, He says this, *"But the Counselor, the Holy Spirit, whom the Father will send in my name, will teach you all things and remind you of everything I have told you."*

God knew those 12 fellas that had been doing life so closely with His Son wouldn't have the ability to remember *every* little thing they learned while they were together.

He also knew it would be totally unrealistic to have them carry around a backpack of scrolls to pull out and reference every time the disciples wondered what they should do in the future.

So, He promised them His Spirit – the unseen substitute who would bring to their remembrance what Jesus had taught them.

This same promise holds true for us today.

Better than any manual, app, or device, the Holy Spirit continually reminds us of truths that God has taught or shown us.

Our Father knew that spiritual amnesia would be an issue for us.

We are forgetful (and easily distracted) beings.

We only have so much mental margin; our lives are demanding; and our brains are assailed on a daily basis with information overload.

The Holy Spirit provides real-time reminders of truth that we need every day.

We don't need to be Bible scholars. We just need to have a willing heart and an attentive spirit.

Lord Jesus, you are the same yesterday, today, and forever. Thank you for your promises that are sure, steadfast, and constant. Please remind me of truths you've already taught me that I need to remember today. Write your word on my heart as you guide me with your Spirit. Amen.

The Table, Our Nemesis, and True Victory

The Lord has said: You will be delivered by returning
and resting; your strength will lie in quiet confidence.
Isaiah 30:15 (NIV)

I was tired.

Tired of the spiritual warfare I found myself in. Tired of the same circumstances bubbling to the forefront of my life. Tired of bringing the same cares and burdens to the Lord.

Just tired.

I opened my Bible to read, *"God prepares a table before me in the presence of my enemies ... "* (Psalm 23:5 CSB)

Such a simple statement.

The problem was I'd been overlooking a key truth in this promise and, as a result, had become weary in fighting the good fight.

God was inviting me to His table – even in the face of opposition.

Life can be hard, can't it?

Daily, we find ourselves navigating heartbreaks, loss, frustrations, illnesses, and the overall tests and trials of living in a broken world filled with broken people.

Overarching all of this is the spiritual warfare we find ourselves engaged in.

If we're not careful, fatigue can set in; weariness can overtake us.

We have an enemy who is actively opposed to us on a daily basis. He is crafty, smart, cunning and will do anything in his power to fracture our faith, destroy our joy, and steal our peace.

It may be a disagreement with our spouse; an irritation with our kids; or a conflict with a coworker at the office.

God, in His wisdom and incredible care, knew that we would need a space to just sit and rest; to come – with all of our hurts, wounds, and scars and just be.

In the presence of our enemies.

God doesn't promise here to take the enemy away; to remove him from our environment; or to send him on his merry way once we sit down at the table.

God invites us to come and sit down at this table *while* our enemy is still lurking and hanging around.

Our victory is found at the table. When we come, sit down, and rest.

Jesus, I come to the table. Please teach me to rest here – in the presence of my enemies; when I'm dealing with loss and pain; when I don't know what to do. I trust that you'll provide abundantly. Amen.

The Waiting isn't Wasted

I wait for the Lord, my soul waits, and in His word I
hope ... Psalm 130:5 (ESV)

Waiting.

It can be so hard, can't it?

I've lost count of the various seasons of waiting God has brought me
through in my life.

Waiting to be married.

Waiting to have children.

Waiting on my dream job.

Waiting for a prodigal to return.

Waiting for reconciliation in a friendship.

Waiting.

None of those waiting seasons have been easy. Because I'm human.

One of the really cool things about God, though, is that He's not human. He sees our lives from beginning to end and has fashioned every season we walk through with intentionality and purpose.

Nothing is wasted.

Nothing.

Every, single minute has meaning and value.

There's something to be learned. Growth to be embraced. Faith to be fostered.

"We know that all things work together for the good of those who love God, who are called according to His purpose." (Romans 8:28 CSB)

All things.

Even the time spent waiting.

So often, we become fixated on what we don't have or don't see instead of what God is actually doing in us and for us in the moment.

With God, there is no such thing as wasted time.

Let's not miss what He's doing today!

Father, waiting can be so hard! Please use the waiting in my life to remove anything that's not of you – in particular, my longing to be in control. I surrender it to you. Help me to see what you're doing in the wait and how you're actively working to help me look more like your Son, Jesus. Amen.

This Hurts

For I consider that the sufferings of this present time are not worth comparing with the glory that is going to be revealed to us. Romans 8:18 (CSB)

Discipline and suffering.

Not many of us read those two words, raise our hands, and shout, *"Yes, please! Sign me up for a double portion of that!"*

The very words discipline and suffering evoke images of pain and discomfort, two things scientifically proven humans will avoid at all cost.

Yet, our days seem to be filled with suffering in some manner, don't they? It might be anything from a broken relationship to a broken appliance; a loss of a loved one to a loss of a job; a longing to be married to a longing for some rest.

Unchecked, suffering can wear us down and cause us to become discouraged and weary.

As Christ-followers, though, we are encouraged to keep discipline and suffering in their proper perspective.

The first 12 verses of Hebrews 12 provide a clear description of how God uses suffering and discipline for our good.

"Endure suffering as discipline...[God] disciplines us for our benefit, so that we can share His holiness." (vs. 7 & 10 CSB)

Discipline is synonymous with training.

We have all heard stories of athletes who disciplined themselves in order to be their very best at their sport. The rigorous diets and workouts, the early morning conditionings, and their regimented daily routines were all part of the training it took to be an amazing athlete.

They disciplined themselves so as to be in shape when it came time to perform.

God uses the suffering in our lives in a similar fashion. We are being trained by it (if we let it), sharpened through it, and challenged to grow and mature to look more like our Savior than we ever have.

Contrary to what the enemy loves to tell us, suffering and discipline are not punishment – God doesn't hate us.

"My dear child, don't shrug off God's discipline, but don't be crushed by it either. It's the child He loves that He disciplines; the child He embraces, He also corrects ...

This trouble [suffering] you're in isn't punishment; it's training, the normal experience of children. Only irresponsible parents would leave children to fend for themselves." (Hebrews 12: 5, 9, and 10 MSG)

What's the purpose of discipline and suffering then? Why do we go through so much of it?

"... it pays off big-time, for it's the well-trained who find themselves mature in their relationship with God." (vs. 10 MSG)

Through suffering, we grow to become mature in our relationship with God, steadfast in our walk, and anchored in our faith.

Jesus, help me lean into you during times of suffering and discipline in my life. Let me see how deeply the Scriptures apply to me, how very rich and deep your love is for me (even in my darkest of moments) and how you are using everything in my life to train and develop me to be stronger in my faith for your glory. Amen.

Wash, Rinse, and Repeat

Remind me each morning of Your constant love, for I put my trust in You. My prayers go up to You; show me the way I should go. Psalm 143:8 (GNT)

I had gotten up a little later than I'd planned.

I raced to the shower, jumped in, and got through it in record time. I threw on my outfit for the day, dried my hair, and was beginning to style it when I realized something was wrong.

My freshly-washed hair wasn't responding favorably to the routine combing, curling, and fluffing that I generally did. No matter what I tried, my hair was just not cooperating.

Then it dawned on me. I had forgotten to shampoo!

(*Insert internal scream here.*)

I didn't have time to do anything about it, so out the door I went.

The result?

All day long, my hair was limp, unmanageable, and downright dismal.

Kind of like my soul is during the day if I don't connect with Jesus first thing in the morning.

I've jumped out of bed and raced out the door enough times in my life to know that, if I don't take some time to chat with my First Love, my soul will be limp; my day, unmanageable; and my attitude, dismal.

Nineteenth Century British pastor, George Mueller, said it best, *"The first great and primary business to which I ought to attend every day is to get my soul happy in the Lord."*

Just like a good shampoo will cleanse the toxins out of my hair, a good heart-to-heart with Jesus first thing in the morning will cleanse the doldrums out of my soul.

Without this internal wash and rinse every day, my heart is at risk of being disconnected from God and the perpetual communion He desires for me to have with Him.

And, I know what awaits me on the other side of my front door – a broken world in need of light and hope; a cunning enemy ready to hurl taunts and lies in my direction; and lost people who need to be introduced to my Savior.

I can't afford to bypass this crucial time each morning.

Because, it's here, as I sit with Jesus and let His love wash over my soul, that I am reminded of how He's made me fresh and clean; blessed me with a brand new day; and has prepared my steps to be a light of hope and joy to those I meet today.

Lord Jesus, I praise you for this new day! I'm so grateful for your mercies that are new every morning. Refresh me with your faithful love so that I can be a vessel of hope to everyone I meet today. Amen.

Do You Have a Flock?

But encourage each other daily ...
Hebrews 3:13 (HCSB)

Have you ever observed Canadian Geese in flight?

If so, you'll understand me when I say it's not a quiet event. It's a noisy affair with honking galore.

Typically flying in a V-formation, the lead goose blazes a trail for those behind him to follow. This point bird takes the brunt of the journey as he slices the wind current first making flight easier for those who are following him.

All the while, the rest of the geese are honking...honking...honking.

Those who study Canadian Geese tell us that this chorus of honking is their way of encouraging one another in flight.

It's as though they're saying to the leader and each other, *"Well done! Keep going! You're doing an amazing job!"*

Without fail, every time I see a group of these talkative birds in flight, I am reminded of God's family and how He calls us to encourage one another.

"Let us look out for one another and encourage each other to love and good works." (Hebrews 10:24 HCSB)

We all know how tough life can be. The various tests and trials that most of us will face during a lifetime are far too numerous to list.

Trying to fly through life alone makes us a sitting duck, easy pickings for the powers of darkness that love to divide, destroy, and wreak havoc.

God calls us to community, to be a part of His family, to find our flock.

It's in these circles of people that we receive the necessary encouragement, support, love, and care to navigate life's challenging journey.

Who is in your life today, dear friend, that is "honking" and cheering you onward? Who is around you that encourages you to keep moving forward knowing that the best is yet to come?

We all need those people in our flock!

Jesus, thank you for your word! Let me be a holy encourager today! Use me to speak life and blessing into the hearts of those around me today. Help me be the flock that somebody needs. Amen.

What to do with Evil

For whatever is born of God overcomes the world; and this is the victory that has overcome the world – our faith. I John 5:4 (NKJV)

We live in a world with no shortage of evil.

Listening to the latest news cycle reminds us of that, doesn't it?

Honestly, though, we don't even need the news because, on a personal level, we are bumping into evil all day, every day.

Ever have someone do you very wrong and seemingly look like they're getting away with it? If we're being honest, I think we all have in some form or fashion.

On the heels of such injustices, evil can slide into our thoughts with a variety of ideas on how to "make it right."

Human nature, right?

Can I just say right here that I am so grateful that God overshadows our human frailty!

In Psalm 37, God gives us a short, but very clear truth to help us navigate this human tendency.

"Turn away from evil, do what is good … " (vs. 27 CSB)

That's generally not what we're inclined to do, is it?

In our brokenness, we tend to stare at evil, fixate on evil, obsess over evil.

Anything but turn away from it!

But God doesn't stop there. He gives us direction, clarity, and something better to do instead.

"… do what is good … "

Our Father knows that doing what is good is, ultimately, what's best for us and those around us.

It leaves evil in the hands of the only One who truly can deal with it effectively.

God.

"Friends, do not avenge yourselves; instead leave room for God's wrath, because it is written, Vengeance belongs to me, I will repay, says the Lord …"

Do not be conquered [overcome] by evil, but conquer [overcome] evil with good." (Romans 12:19 & 21 CSB)

Jesus, I give you this struggle today. My flesh wants to focus on ways that I've been wronged or get frustrated when I see evil at work in the world. I surrender this temptation to you and ask you to help me busy myself with doing good for your Kingdom. Amen.

Beyond My Reach but Not My Prayers

Pray without ceasing. I Thessalonians 5:17 (ESV)

My husband and I are empty-nesters.

The days of making little lunches, working through endless piles of laundry, and juggling a variety of extracurricular activities are over.

Our four children are all grown and living their own independent lives and I smile to see them happily settling into their own marriages, careers, and families.

As parents, though, that transition can be challenging, can't it?

We spend decades providing for them, instructing them, and ultimately, preparing them to leave us and our homes.

Yet, when the time finally comes for them to vacate the nest, we sometimes struggle to understand what our new role is.

Many times, we try to continue to be a remote extension of what we once were when they lived in our house. As a result, we insert ourselves where we're not invited; offer advice when it's not solicited; and try to co-manage their decisions and jump in to offer damage control if we see things not going so well.

Speaking from experience, that generally doesn't help.

The book of Job offers a wonderful example of how we, as parents, can continue to influence the lives of our children for good, even when they're grown, out of our homes, and making their own decisions.

Job's sons *"used to take turns having banquets at their homes"* and would invite their sisters to join them. (Job 1:4 CSB)

There's no record of Job attending these house parties, however *"whenever a round of banqueting was over, Job would send for his children and purify them, rising early in the morning to offer burnt offerings for all of them."*

"For Job thought, 'Perhaps my children have sinned, having cursed God in their hearts.' This was Job's regular practice." (vs. 5)

Even as an empty-nester, Job continued to spiritually cover his grown children in prayer. He continued to exercise his God-given parental authority to bring his kids before God's throne regardless of their age or station in life.

Can you think of anything more influential than this?

Our children will grow up, move out, and embark on their own lives. Our days of in-home nurturing will come to a close.

But the truth that should comfort every parent's heart is simply this – while your children will eventually be beyond your reach, they will never be beyond your prayers!

Lord Jesus, I lift my children up to you – no matter what age they are! Please draw them into a closer relationship with you. Show up strong in their lives and reveal yourself in a deeper way to them today. Keep them under the shadow of your wings all the days of their lives and anchor their hearts in your truth always. Amen.

Sometimes Things Get Worse After Praying

That day Pharaoh commanded the overseers of the people as well as their foremen: 'Don't continue to supply the people with straw for making bricks, as before. They must go and gather straw for themselves. But require the same quota of bricks ... as before ... they are slackers ... ' Exodus 5:6-8 (CSB)

One of the things I love most about the Bible is how we can take the stories written on those crisp pages, lay them over our own lives, and see ourselves so clearly in the application.

An all-time favorite of mine is Moses. If you are living and breathing right now, then you can definitely find yourself somewhere in the ups and downs of any one of his life's adventures.

Here's a perfect example ...

How many times have you prayed for something to improve only to discover it seemingly got worse?

That happened to Moses!

After having his initial chat with God about delivering the children of Israel from their slavery in Egypt, Moses set out to do just that.

The simplicity of his mission was before him – free God's people from bondage and lead them into the promised land.

When he got to Pharaoh, however, he was met with hardened resistance. Worse yet, the heavy work load that the children of Israel had been suffering under was *increased* after Moses confronted Pharaoh.

The children of Israel were horrified and made a beeline to Moses in anger.

"May the Lord take note of you and judge ... " (Exodus 5:21)

Can you imagine how bamboozled Moses must have been? The children of Israel just went from the frying pan to the fire!

This didn't look anything like what God had promised. Moses went to bat for God's people and things got much worse!

Of course, we know what happens next. Right around the corner was the Red Sea and the miraculous deliverance that God had planned.

But they didn't know that. They couldn't see past their crushing circumstances.

Maybe you can relate?

How many times have you found yourself frustrated or angry at God because things seemed to get worse after you prayed?

We don't generally see the big picture. But God does. And His promises remain true even when it looks like the Pharaohs in our lives have only increased our suffering.

He *"is the same yesterday and today and forever."* (Hebrews 13:8 CSV)

The same God who had the Red Sea deliverance ready for His people then is the same God who has a perfect plan in place and ready for you today.

Jesus, help me trust you when circumstances feel like they're falling apart. Help me rest in your promises when things appear to not be getting any better. I believe that you see me and that you care for me and love me more than I can comprehend. I trust that you have fashioned my steps and have prepared for me a good hope and a future. Amen.

Purposefully Different but Essential

But as it is, God has arranged each one of the parts in the body just as He wanted. I Corinthians 12:18 (CSB)

I heard them before I saw them.

Barking wildly, a team of eight dogs, lashed together, came whipping around the snow-packed corner. Pulling a sled with a driver behind them, this team of beautiful huskies slowed as the "musher" brought them to a well-trained stop.

Will, our seasoned dogsled guide in the Colorado Rockies, waved our small group over and began our session by introducing us to each of the dogs.

As he did, he also explained their roles on the team.

I was in awe listening to him describe each of the dog's positions because they were all very unique. Two huskies were placed in the lead, point, team, and wheel positions, respectively, with very specific tasks to execute.

If just one dog didn't do its part, the whole team would fail.

I couldn't help but think about how God purposefully places each of us right where we fit best.

Just like the dogsled trainers handpick very specific dogs for each of these essential roles, God intentionally chooses where He positions each of us on His team (in His body of believers).

I Corinthians 12 details how God's body – His Church – is made up of a variety of people, bringing unique strengths and gifts to it.

He purposefully chooses where to place us because, ultimately, He knows exactly how He made us, where we will most thrive, and what is best for the whole team (His Church).

In dogsledding, the success of the team depends greatly on whether the right dogs are placed into each vital position.

Isn't that also true of the roles we hold in life? In our families, our professions, and our church?

The question is, do you see your divinely assigned position as essential?

It can be easy to look around and covet someone else's position in life because they look more popular, affluent, put-together, gifted, or polished (especially on social media).

But, just like in dogsledding, one position isn't more important than another.

They are different. But all are essential.

We are all different, but we are all essential.

That's such a powerful truth!

Our Father is supremely aware that His children who make up His body represent all walks of life and bring unique perspectives to help others around them connect to life in Christ.

We need each other. God made us that way and He strategically and purposefully places us precisely where He wants us to be on His team so that we can do the most good.

Lord Jesus, I praise you for this truth! What an honor it is to be part of your forever family. Help me to use my gifts, talents, calling, and experiences today to help the body of Christ and, ultimately, glorify you. Amen.

This Weight is Heavy

... God is faithful; He will not allow you to be
tempted beyond what you are able, but ... will provide
a way out so that you may be able to bear it.
I Corinthians 10:13 (CSB)

Weightlifting.

Besides Arnold Schwarzenegger, The Rock, and my husband, is
there *really* anyone else on the planet who enjoys this activity?

The very idea of stressing your muscles to the point of exhaustion
and pain is not my idea of fun (and, of course, "fun" should be a
prerequisite for any activity or task, in my opinion).

However, watching my husband's discipline over the years has given me a deep appreciation for what he's working to do – be physically healthy and strong.

It's also given me the opportunity to understand God and His wisdom a little bit better.

Countless times in my Christian journey, I have faced my own spiritual weight bench while walking through deeply painful circumstances. My prayers felt futile and my faith weak.

A failed first marriage that ended in divorce leaving me with fragile security and identity issues. A child who went prodigal for several years causing me to wrestle with internal doubts and fears.

Friendships that became fractured and frayed over the years leaving me to wonder if there was more I should have done to salvage them.

Those examples (and so many more) were filled with crushing guilt, unbearable shame, and waves of darkness that drove me to my knees.

But it was through those deeply trying and extremely challenging situations that God grew my faith.

The spiritual weight increased; the burden intensified; my faith muscles were challenged in order to grow stronger.

You see, if we are never met with resistance, we remain puny. Faith weaklings.

It's *in* the trials, the siftings, and the hardships that our faith muscles are pushed and made to grow. It's *through* our most difficult seasons that we mature in our faith the most.

"Consider it great joy, my brothers and sisters, whenever you experience various trials, because you know that the testing of your faith produces endurance … let endurance have its full effect, so that you may be mature and complete, lacking nothing." (James 1:2-4 CSB)

So, the next time you find yourself doing some spiritual heavy lifting, don't quit! Know that God is working to grow some healthy, strong faith in you!

Jesus, help me not shy away from this truth. Fill me with courage as I encounter various tests and trials. Help me to remember that spiritual resistance is being used to develop and grow me to look more like you. Strengthen my faith so that I do not faint. You are my strength, my hope, and my joy. Amen.

Not My Job

Jesus said, 'You're not in charge here. The Father who sent me is in charge. He draws people to Me ... then I do My work, putting people together, setting them on their feet ... ' John 6:44 (MSG)

I'm so grateful I don't have the Holy Spirit's job.

It's a real struggle to remember that sometimes, though. There have been many occasions when I've tried to give Him a hand and help Him out only to fail miserably in my human attempts.

I can't change anyone. None of us can.

But that's not always easy to remember, is it?

As badly as we may want to, change is something that only the Holy Spirit can put His finger on and help any of us embrace.

We all have blind spots. We all have areas in which we need to grow, change, or even repent of, but it's the work of the Holy Spirit who ultimately illuminates us to see these needs and then softens our hearts to cooperate with God in the process.

It's heartbreaking, though, to see people we love and care for unable to overcome an addiction or struggle with relationship difficulties. It's awful to see those we care about collapse under the weight of an unsustainable schedule or teeter on the precipice of divorce.

Our natural inclination is to jump in and offer words of helpful advice. Steps they can take, ways they can fix it, or things we think they should do differently.

Then, when we see our "encouragement" disregarded or blatantly ignored, it can be a temptation to turn up the heat, say it again, or get angry because they just don't seem to be listening.

But conviction is not something we can orchestrate. No matter how hard we try.

The Holy Spirit is the only One who knows when the timing is the best, the circumstances are perfect, and the individual's heart is ready.

"... I will send (the Holy Spirit) to you ... when He comes, He will convict the world about (the guilt of) sin (and the need for a Savior) ... " (John 16:7 & 8 AMP)

This places the burden of responsibility squarely on His shoulders, not ours.

Which frees us up to trust.

Trust that God is able to do all things – even if the temporary looks like it's going up in flames.

Trust that His timing is perfect – no matter how hard it feels in the moment.

Trust that He is enough – He is more than capable and loves those individuals we care for more deeply than we do.

Jesus, thank you for the ministry of the Holy Spirit. Forgive me for the times I've tried to do his job. Lord, I release the situations, the circumstances, and the people to you right now that I've tried to control and ask that your will would be done. You are the mountain-mover, the chain-breaker, and storm-calmer. Have your way! Amen.

A Broken Family, Forgiveness, and Sunshine

That all of them may be one, Father, just as you are in me and I am in you. May they also be in us so that the world may believe that you have sent me.
John 17:21 (NIV)

She came into my life at the age of five when Anthony and I married. Spunky, radiant, and absolutely full-of-life, Annah quickly became the sunshine of our freshly blended family unit.

She saw the bright side of everything and wanted nothing more than to have a mommy who loved her and a tightly-knit family under one roof.

Her hopes were pure and I admired her bouncy, pigtail-infused enthusiasm.

But the raw truth was, I wasn't really excited about the prospect of "starting over" – my biological children were already teenagers and didn't require my constant attention.

This little five-year-old would.

May I be vulnerable?

There were many times I wrestled to be present in the moment for Annah and caused her little heart to quietly wonder if I cared.

On countless occasions, I struggled to show her affection which caused her to privately question my love.

And there were more times than I can count where I hurried through interactions and conversations with her which caused her to internally doubt her worth.

I regret every single one of those moments.

However, here's the incredible, life-giving truth that I pray breathes hope into someone's heart reading this today ...

God redeemed it all.

One day at a time, one apology at a time, so that now, years later, you'd be hard pressed to tell that she and I got our start in a blended family.

How can such a transformation be possible?

In the book of Matthew, Peter asked Jesus the question, *"How many times should I forgive my brother or sister who sins against me? As many as seven times?"*

Jesus responded with an answer that, I dare say, challenges most of us today, *"I tell you not as many as seven, but seventy times seven."* (Matthew 18:21-22 CSB)

That's a whole lot of forgiveness going on every single day! And in a broken, blended family, forgiveness is essential.

In order to get where we are now, Annah and I needed to grab hold of God's abundant grace each day; extend forgiveness and love routinely; and be willing to engage in some open and honest communication (that didn't always feel good).

Of course, this truth goes far beyond just blended family dynamics. Any relationship worth having requires work.

The question is how badly do we want what Jesus promises us we can have? (John 17:21)

Jesus, thank you for being such a wonderful Savior and modeling what true forgiveness looks like. Forgive me for the times I've been unwilling to humble myself and ask for forgiveness – from you and others. Help me to follow your example, be clothed in your humility, and be willing to work on my relationships so that they reflect the Gospel and point others to you. Amen.

Church Hurt is Real

... not neglecting to gather together, as some are in the habit of doing ... Hebrews 10:25 (CSB)

Church hurt is real.

As someone who has spent her life in church, I can say that with certainty.

But, here's the thing ... God wants us to be in community, benefitting from the mutual faith and encouragement of other Christ-followers.

So, how do we reconcile the two?

The simple fact is that, this side of Heaven, there is *no* perfect church. Zip. Nada. Zilch.

Churches are made up of broken people the same as any other organization, industry, or group.

What sets church apart is the Gospel.

The Good News that Jesus's death on the cross is able to make anyone new (2 Corinthians 5:17); infuse hope into our lives (Jeremiah 29:11); and redeem us from the grave (Psalm 49:15).

And church staff, volunteers, and attenders alike all need the Gospel.

For Christ-followers, we're instructed to not forsake this necessary time in community.

Why?

So we can *"... watch out for one another to provoke love and good works ... encouraging each other, and all the more as you see the Day approaching."* (Hebrews 10:24-25 CSB)

We need each other. We need others in our lives who will encourage us, help us in our walk with Jesus, and remind us of how to get love right.

Will offenses happen? Absolutely. We're sinful people in need of God's forgiveness, mercy, and grace on a daily basis.

Does it change God's heart for us to be in community? No.

Because it's here, in community – broken, messy, and sometimes painful community – that God uses other believing, Gospel-minded people to help us grow and look more like Jesus in our own faith journeys.

If you find yourself wrestling with church hurt today, I pray that you would first give it to God. He sees and understands better than anyone. (Remember, Jesus was also hurt by the church and religious leaders of His day.)

Then, ask Him to show you your community. What church is best for you? What small group is right for you?

He knows. He'll show you.

Resist the temptation to let church hurt keep you from Jesus and the life-giving community we all were created to need.

Lord Jesus, you know my story. You've fashioned my days and have been with me through every single one. You're aware of the hurt and the scars in my life caused by church, it's leadership, or people I've encountered there. I can't change any of it. I surrender it all to you. Help me to trust you today and be obedient to plug into a Gospel-centered community that is life-giving to me. Let me also be life-giving to it. Amen.

Fear's Silver Lining

Fear not, for I am with you; be not dismayed, for I am your God. Isaiah 41:10 (NKJV)

Fear.

It can stop us in our tracks, can't it?

Many of us have heard there are 365 "don't fear" references in the Bible – one for every day of the year, conveniently.

But, what if we *do* fear?

If we find ourselves struggling with it – for a moment, a day, a season – will God be disappointed in us? Angry with us?

Judges 6 tells the story of a man named Gideon. Referred to as a *"valiant warrior"* in verse 12. Gideon seemed anything but brave and courageous just a few verses later.

God asked Gideon to get rid of a couple idols in town and build an altar to God there instead.

" ... tear down the altar of Baal that belongs to your father and cut down the Asherah pole beside it. Build a well-constructed altar to the Lord your God on the top of this mound." (vs. 25-26)

Gideon was willing ... and afraid.

"... because he was too afraid of his father's family and the men of the city to do it in the daytime, he did it at night." (vs. 27)

I find that so relatable, don't you?

And, if you continue reading through Judges 6, you'll see that fear can actually have a silver lining.

It made Gideon desperate.

Gideon became desperate for strength from beyond himself to lead an army into battle. He was desperate for courage that he knew he didn't humanly possess and desperate for direction from the only One who could truly give it.

Gideon's fear made him desperate for God.

The same holds true for us.

Fear can be a great motivator to spur us towards dependency on God. It can bring us to our knees and can be instrumental in growing our faith, if we let it.

"Jesus, I need you ... "

"Father, without you I can't ... "

"O Lord, you know I'm afraid ... "

Even Jesus Himself was no stranger to fear. It drove Him to pray several times the night before He was crucified. (Matthew 26:36-44)

Hebrews 4:15 tells us He is able *" ... to sympathize and understand our weaknesses and temptations ... (because He) has been tempted [knowing exactly how it feels to be human] in every respect as we are ... "* (AMP)

And, because we have a Savior who knows what fear feels like, He urges us to come and bring our fears to Him so He can help us.

"Let us then approach God's throne of grace with confidence, so that we may receive mercy and find grace to help us in our time of need." (Hebrews 4:16 NIV)

Jesus, I'm so grateful you know what fear feels like and that you invite me to bring you all of my fears and lay them down at your feet. I give them to you now. Please exchange my fears with divine courage and the boldness to take you at your word knowing that you are with me always. Amen.

Giant-Slaying Tips

For the battle is not yours, but God's.
2 Chronicles 20:15 (NIV)

Most of us have heard the story of David and Goliath before.

The story is ripe with parallels to our own lives, and David's example truly offers us some premier tips on how to slay those persistent giants that we periodically have to contend with!

Because we all face Goliaths, don't we? They may not be 9-foot plus, armor-clad warriors, but they're giants nonetheless.

Circumstances that appear daunting and insurmountable; people that are continuously challenging; or situations that deeply test our faith can all be giants.

Giants are intimidating (I Samuel 17:3-7); they block forward progress (vs. 8-11); and they take time to deal with (vs. 16).

What's more, if you read through the story, you'll discover that David didn't exactly appear to be the best guy for this job (something I'm sure we can all sympathize with when we're standing toe-to-toe with our own giants)!

David's resume was short and "giant-slayer" was nowhere in his work history.

He was the youngest of eight brothers; just a youth and a lowly shepherd (vs. 12-15).

His three oldest brothers were already on the battlefield with more military experience (vs. 13).

King Saul, Israel's Commander in Chief, questioned David's ability to help (vs. 33).

But, with the odds stacked against him (not to mention people's opinions), David stepped up to face Goliath with divine confidence because he saw what the others weren't seeing.

The heart.

David didn't fixate on Goliath "the giant" like everyone else. He honed-in on Goliath's heart and the ugly things that were pouring out of it – offensive taunts, lies, and accusations being hurled against God and His people.

This empowered David to act and speak with divine confidence, conviction, and faith (vs. 45-47).

Right before charging towards Goliath with nothing more than his courage, a sling and a few stones, David loudly declared, "... *the battle is the Lord's. He will hand you over* ... "(vs. 47)

The rest, as they say, is history. Goliath was defeated that day at the hands of a faith-filled shepherd boy.

To those around him, including Goliath, David looked weak and insignificant.

He appeared to be standing alone without anyone else cheering for him or believing he would make it out of that predicament alive.

But David understood that it wasn't *his* fight. It was God's.

And, as a result, David placed his confidence – and his life – squarely in God's hands.

It doesn't matter if we feel capable, qualified, supported, or equipped. All that matters is that we remember the battle belongs to the Lord and leave the rest up to Him.

Father, thank you for the story of David and Goliath. Thank you for David's example of faith, courage, and conviction recorded for our encouragement. I give you my giants today, Lord Jesus! Help me remember the battle is yours, not mine. Teach me to embrace my day with divine confidence and surrender every giant to you! Amen.

This is the day that the Lord has made.
Let us rejoice and be glad in it.

Psalm 118:24 (HCSB)

It's a new day …
Thank You, Jesus, for Your mercies and kindness.
Thank You for Your unwavering love.
Thank You for never giving up on me.
(Lamentations 3:22-23)

It's a new day …
Help me to pick up my cross and follow You,
Not because it's easy or popular
But because it's good and right.
(Matthew 16:24-26)

It's a new day …
Help me to see people through Your eyes,
Respond to people like You would,
And love them like You do.
(I John 4:19-21)

It's a new day …
I choose to lay all my cares at Your feet.
Help me not pick them up again.
You are the only One strong enough to carry them.
(I Peter 5:7)

It's a new day …
Use me to encourage someone today;
To show them who You really are, Jesus,
And to reflect Your heart in a meaningful way.
(Hebrews 10:24-25)

It's a new day …
Please fill me with Your Spirit;
Arm me with Your Word;
Surround me with Your favor.
(Galatians 5:22-23; Psalm 5:12)

It's a new day …
I surrender all.
I choose You.
I love You.
(John 15:5)

Sitting in the Dark

But you, Lord, are a shield around me, my glory, and the
One who lifts up my head. Psalms 3:3 (CSB)

Dark days. We all have them.

You know the ones – when reading your Bible feels pointless; every
fiber of your being feels blah; and God seems like He's a gazillion miles
away focusing on anything but you.

They're awful, terrible, no-good days and I had one recently.

Several heavy life circumstances had collided at once creating the
perfect storm for my soul.

The thought of steamrolling through a variety of chores and tasks just to distract myself until I felt better crossed my mind.

I've done that many times before, though, and knew the results would be shallow, superficial, and quite temporary.

Like putting a band-aid on a C-section. Completely ineffective.

Instead, I was reminded of what David modeled in the Psalms.

Waiting patiently.

Not a popular option, I know, and one that our flesh tends to recoil from on every level.

But, look at what happens to the soul who's willing to do so ...

"I waited patiently for the Lord, and He turned to me and heard my cry for help.

He brought me up from a desolate pit, out of the muddy clay, and set my feet on a rock, making my steps secure.

He put a new song in my mouth ... " (Psalms 40:1-3 CSB)

This isn't a passive kind of waiting.

David placed himself in a posture of expectancy. He realized that there was no human effort on his part that would help. He was desperate for divine insight, movement, and deliverance.

Have you ever felt that way? Desperate. Stuck. Sitting in the dark.

Maybe you do today?

The same God who met David in his moments of darkness is the same God who meets and helps us today.

He sees and hears us.

He lifts us out of the darkness and rescues us from that desolate, isolated pit that wants to hold our soul hostage.

He shines His light and helps us get unstuck.

He renews our joy and restores our peace.

He brings us to that place where we can say like David did – *"[He] answered me!"* (Psalms 22:21 CSB)

Lord Jesus, I admit I don't wait patiently very well. Honestly, I've expected you to immediately fix those times when I've felt stuck. Please forgive me. Your ways are higher than my ways and I know that you see my path better than I do and are leading me in the best way for my good. Teach me to wait patiently. With peace and joy. Believing that you see me and are already working to help. Amen.

The Potter is Kind to the Clay

Lord, You are our Father; we are the clay, and You
are our potter; we all are the work of Your hands.
Isaiah 64:8 (CSB)

We were greeted warmly at the door.

My friend, a potter by trade, had opened her studio up and was excited to teach a handful of folks – myself included – how to make a mug.

We all exchanged introductions and quickly donned our aprons to begin.

After getting started, it became abundantly apparent to me that this was not as easy as my friend made it look.

My novice hands were nowhere near as seasoned as hers.

As she patiently and gently shaped the rim of her mug, I was struggling to make mine form the shape of a basic circle.

I eventually asked her why we couldn't just pinch or squeeze the rim into shape. It seemed like it would be quicker.

She smiled kindly and began to explain, "Clay doesn't respond well to pressure or force. It requires a continuous, gentle molding to shape it into what you want it to become."

And that's the moment when the Holy Spirit whispered to me, *"Just like God does with you."*

As Christ-followers, we are likened to clay that God is continuously molding and shaping.

If you're anything like me, though, you've probably anticipated this shaping process to include severity, harshness, and pressure.

So many times, I've braced myself for His molding of me to include squashing, smashing, squeezing, or pinching.

Yet, this is not at all in line with the character of our beloved Father, the Master Potter.

He is patient and kind as He gently molds us into the shape He intends for us to take.

There's no unkindness in His shaping; no harshness as He goes over places in our lives that need repetition.

He doesn't grow weary, get angry, or walk away when we have spots that require a little more work.

His hands continuously work to smooth out our jagged edges, soften down our wayward tendencies, and help us to become beautiful vessels He can use for His glory.

We are His workmanship and, *"I am sure of this, that He who began a good work in (us) will bring it to completion at the day of Jesus Christ."* (Philippians 1:6ESV)

Lord God, I'm so grateful you love me enough to continue to work on me. Thank you for your kindness and love as you shape me to look more like you today than ever before. I yield to the gentle work of your hands in my life and ask that you would continue to mold and shape me into a beautiful vessel for your glory. Amen.

Wasn't My Love Enough?

I know that You can do anything and no plan of Yours can be thwarted. Job 42:2 (CSB)

I don't think there's anything that can aptly prepare a parent to navigate a season with a prodigal child.

I've never met a parent yet who would knowingly sign up for such a trial.

For me, watching my child walk out the door with nothing but a backpack to her name and a willful defiance in her heart was the most horrifying, heartbreaking, gut-wrenching day I've ever lived through.

Partly because I knew that everything she was running toward would only leave her more empty than she already was and partly because I couldn't help but question where I went wrong as a parent.

As a Christ-follower, I thought I'd done everything right. I took my daughter to church, prayed with and for her, taught her about Jesus, read the Bible with her and tried to live it out on a daily basis.

I did my utmost to be present in her life and had tried to raise her as best I knew how.

Which left me with the nagging question: *Wasn't my love enough?*

If my love was enough, surely she would never have wanted to leave her family, abandon her faith, and run headlong into the arms of a very broken world.

But the truth was that my love was *not* enough ... and never would be.

Because it was never about my love. It was about His.

(Talk about an eye-opening revelation that cut straight through this Momma's self-righteous heart!)

I had been given the privilege of raising this child, but saving her was something I could never possibly do.

I had put my confidence in my ability to parent and, ultimately, my works. Without realizing it, I had ignorantly missed the very truth that God wanted me to hang onto as a parent – He is sovereign.

Only God, through numerous demonstrations of *His* unfailing love, can save our children, pursue them with a divine passion that is eternal, and beckon their hearts with a mercy that invites them to surrender all.

Human love is wonderful, but it can only go so far. It can never save, provide, or comfort in the way that God can.

No matter how hard I loved my daughter, it was never going to be enough to save her. Only Jesus could do that.

And, the good news is, He did.

Jesus, forgive me for thinking in any way that I am somehow responsible to save my children. You created them and, ultimately, you save them. I lift my children up to you now and ask that you would capture their hearts. Help them to fall in love with you, stay in love with you, and grow in relationship with you. Be their God, now and forever. Amen.

My Imperfect Marriage

Jesus said, "If anyone wants to follow after me, let
him deny himself, take up his cross, and follow me."
Matthew 16:24 (CSV)

I don't even remember what started it now.

We were just a few minutes into a conversation recently before Anthony and I found ourselves in a tiff that left me emotionally crinkled and somewhat frustrated.

I walked out of the room and prayed these exact words, *"God, help me love an imperfect man!"*

The vehement statement had barely escaped my lips before the Holy Spirit tapped me on the shoulder and handed me a mirror.

As crinkled as I was, I couldn't help but chuckle.

With more than two decades of marriage under our belt now, Anthony and I don't tend to have as many verbal jousting matches as we did when we were newly married.

However, we're both still broken people in need of God's forgiveness, grace, and mercy on a daily basis. We're not immune to misunderstandings, hurt feelings, or selfish preferences.

We still have a need for the Gospel to be actively working in our marriage because we're both still learning to look and be more like Jesus every day.

Which means there are still hard moments and hard days.

Paul bluntly addressed those choosing to marry in I Corinthians 7 by saying, *"... such people will have trouble in this life ... "* (vs. 28 CSV)

Would we grow in Christ, though, if that wasn't the case?

True growth, healthy growth requires adversity. Challenge. Opposition.

In marriage and in life.

The goal, however, is to always let the adversity drive us closer to Jesus. Because it's there, when we run to Him over and over and over again, that we get to know Him better and better.

We also begin to see ourselves – our sin, brokenness, flaws, failures, and imperfections – clearer and clearer, which is enormously helpful! Because then we can continuously lay them at Jesus's feet, pick up our cross, die (again) to ourselves, and keep following Him.

It's a foundational truth to living the abundant life God has given to us so freely.

Makes me grateful for an imperfect marriage that points me to a perfect Savior every day!

Jesus, thank you for the different relationships in my life that you use to help me look more like you. Teach me to look in the holy mirror of your word whenever I'm frustrated. Lead me to examine my heart instead of being quick to point fingers or cast blame. I need you. Today and always. Amen.

Forgiven and Loved So Much

You have chosen what is foolish in the world
to shame the wise, and You have chosen what
is weak in the world to shame the strong.
I Corinthians 1:27 (CSB)

Going against the flow isn't easy.

Generally, it's much simpler to keep your head down, do your best

to fit in, and cater to the crowd, isn't it?

But what if that's not God's best for us?

There was a woman in Luke 7 who took going against the flow to another level entirely and glorified God in a way many of us would blush over from embarrassment.

Jesus had been invited to a Pharisee's house for dinner (vs. 36).

When this woman heard Jesus was there, she showed up with an *"alabaster jar of perfume and stood behind him at His feet, weeping, and began to wash His feet with her tears.*

She wiped His feet with her hair, kissing them and anointing them with the perfume." (vs. 37-38)

The Pharisee watched. His internal reaction was immediate...and critical.

He knew this woman was a "sinner" and was appalled that Jesus would permit such a person into His presence much less allow this emotional and disruptive display to take place (vs. 39).

The woman had a past, littered with choices she regretted.

Her decision to crash the Pharisee's dinner party and act like a fool in the presence of everyone was an intentional act of thanksgiving and worship.

She knew she was a sinner.

She was aware of her reputation.

She could feel the Pharisee's judgmental gaze.

None of that mattered in that moment.

Her life had been redeemed.

She was here, at the Pharisee's dinner party, because of love.

The Pharisee saw her actions as foolish.

Jesus saw them as worship.

He used the opportunity to share a story with the Pharisee (that, ultimately, contrasted her seemingly over-the-top public display to the Pharisee's strict adherence to behavioral norms).

And, as was the pattern of Jesus, He boiled it all down to the heart, *"Therefore I tell you, her many sins have been forgiven; that's why she loved much. But the one who is forgiven little, loves little."* (vs. 47)

This woman knew she had been "forgiven of much" and, as a result, her actions conveyed it – even when they weren't socially acceptable.

I wonder if we can say the same?

Jesus, let me remember how very much I am forgiven and loved! Help me pour that love out on others today and be willing, if need be, to look like a fool in the eyes of the world as I glorify and worship you, my precious King. Amen.

About the Author

Kristen West can't remember a time that words weren't a part of her life.

As a girl, she remembers the library being more fun than the playground. Getting to buy books in school though the Scholastic Book order program was better than free candy.

Words were so influential to her during her formative years that, by the time she was in high school, speaking competitively on the school's Forensic Team felt natural.

College was filled with as many writing, speaking, and literature classes as she could pack into her schedule. After receiving her degree in Journalism, she went on to write feature stories for a hometown newspaper.

Coming to Christ in her late-teens, her natural love for words united with a divine passion to encourage, inspire, and challenge others in their personal faith journeys.

A lover of true stories, her three devotion-style books weave some of her own personal stories of how God has shown up in her life with Biblical principles and practical application.

Kristen loves to travel often, visit small coffee shops frequently, and watch new sunrises every morning.

You can follow Kristen and connect with her by going to:

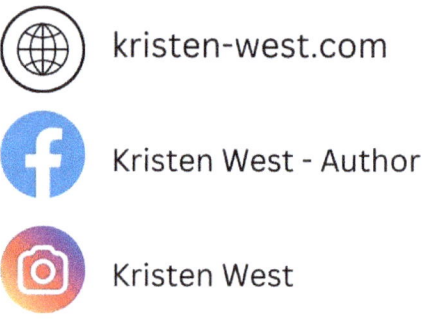

kristen-west.com

Kristen West - Author

Kristen West